bodymatters

WHY WON'T KIM
eat?
Janine amos

CHERRYTREE BOOKS

bodymatters
Kate Smokes Cigarettes
Jon Drinks Alcohol
Why Won't Kim Eat?
Is Helen Pregnant?
Alex Does Drugs
Jamal is Overweight

A Cherrytree Book

First published 2002
by Cherrytree Press
327 High Street
Slough
Berkshire
SL1 1TX

© Evans Brothers Limited 2002

British Library Cataloguing in Publication Data

Amos, Janine
Why won't Kim eat? - (Bodymatters)
1. Eating disorders - Juvenile literature
I. Title
616.8'526

ISBN 184234109X

Printed in Hong Kong by Wing King Tong Co Ltd

Acknowledgements
Planning and production: Discovery Books
Editor: Patience Coster
Photographer: David Simson
Designer: Keith Williams
Artwork: Fred van Deelen
Consultant: Dr Gillian Rice

**All the characters appearing in this book
are played by models.**

Picture acknowledgements
The publisher would like to thank
the following for permission to
reproduce their pictures: Popperfoto/Reuters
5, 23, 29; Wellcome Trust Photo Library 15.

WHY WON'T KIM
eat?

contents

It's Saturday afternoon, and Claire is at her friend Kim's house.

4

'Come on, Kim! Put those books away. It's the weekend!' she says.

'OK,' says Kim, frowning. 'I just wanted to start on my maths homework. I'm sure I won't understand all the questions.'

'You're brilliant at maths! Forget about school for a while,' Claire replies happily. 'Let's go and look at the shops!'

On the way into town, the two girls chat about Kim's big sister, Angie. She's getting married in the spring.

'It's going to be a really posh wedding – aren't you excited?' Claire asks.

Kim nods. 'I'll miss Angie, though,' she says sadly. 'It will be really weird at home without her.' Kim and Claire head for their favourite clothes shop.

'What do you think of this?' asks Kim, grabbing a skinny-rib top. 'I could wear it with my new jeans.'

'You'd have to be really slim to wear that!' laughs Claire.

'Maybe I'll g

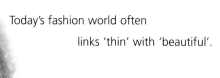

Today's fashion world often links 'thin' with 'beautiful'.

Slimming diets

A slimming diet means eating less food than your body needs, in order to lose weight. Slimming diets are very common in many countries today. People of all weights are trying to become slimmer. Many believe themselves to be overweight when they are not.

Fashion models and TV personalities are often thin. Newspapers, magazines and television all seem to tell us that 'slim is good'. A huge amount of money is spent every day on advertising slimming products and low-fat meals.

In the 1950s, actresses with curvy figures were thought to have an ideal female shape. Today many actresses and models have extremely slim figures. Fashions have changed – and they could change again tomorrow.

n a diet,' says Kim.

As usual, Carol, Kim's mum, is only having salad. 'I'm trying to lose a few pounds!' she laughs, waving away the potatoes.

After the meal, Mum, Dad and Angie sit around the table making wedding plans. Kim is still worried about her homework. 'I'll go and finish my maths,' she says, picking up her bag.

As Kim reaches the door her dad, Joe, turns to smile at her.

'Wow, Kim, those jeans are tight! You'd better not put on any more weight before Angie's big day!' he says, teasing her.

'Right. It's definitely diet time for me!' Kim tells herself, as she slips out of the room.

Later on, Kim feels like a snack. On her way past the sitting room she hears Carol and Joe talking. It sounds as if Carol is crying. Kim stands still, listening.

'What will we do?' sobs Carol. 'Angie's leaving – and in a few years it will be Kim's turn. It will be so lonely with just the two of us.' Kim can feel her heart beating fast. She scuttles past the door and back to her bedroom.

'Don't worry, Mum,' thinks Kim. 'I'll be around for a while yet.'

Kim sits in her

the food Kim eats passes into her stomach

food that cannot be used by Kim's body passes to her large intestine and out of her body as waste

stomach

the food passes from Kim's stomach to her small intestine

ood in the body

When Kim feels hungry, she eats. After she has swallowed the food, muscles push it down into her stomach. The food is helped on its way by the water Kim drinks. After the food has been in Kim's stomach for between two and five hours it moves into her small intestine.

Powerful chemicals called enzymes and a liquid called bile get to work on the food. They begin to change it and break it down so that Kim's body can use it. This process is called digestion. When Kim's food has been digested it can pass through the walls of her small intestine and into her blood. Food that Kim's body can't use passes out as waste when she goes to the toilet.

Food is made up of different parts, or nutrients. This mix of nutrients digested by Kim and carried in her blood gives her energy, helps her to grow and keeps her healthy.

room feeling sad and anxious inside.

?

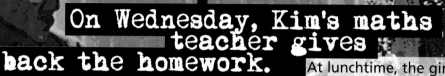

On Wednesday, Kim's maths teacher gives back the homework.

Kim has made one mistake. She feels sick and angry.

'I knew I wouldn't get it right!' says Kim at the end of the lesson.

Claire tries to cheer her up. 'I got six questions wrong!' she says. 'You can't be perfect all the time.'

But Kim is cross with herself. She slams her maths book shut. Three boys in their class turn to look at Kim.

'Chill out, Chubby!' one tells her. 'Give us a smile!'

At lunchtime, the girls sit together. Kim has her head down.

'You're not still worried about the maths are you?' Claire asks her.

Kim sighs. 'It's everything,' she says sadly. 'Everything's going wrong lately. I wish Angie wasn't leaving home. I wish everything would just stay the same.'

Claire opens a packet of crisps from her lunchbox and offers them to Kim.

'No thanks,' says Kim, nibbling on a carrot. 'I'm on a diet until Angie's wedding. I want to be a size ten. Maybe I'll get that right! No one's going to call *me* Chubby again!'

Claire watches as Kim puts her sandwiches into the bin.

Carbohydrates such as bread and potatoes give Kim energy ——

Fats found in foods such as milk, cheese and eggs help to keep Kim's body warm ——

the importance
of food

The nutrients that Kim's body needs are called proteins, fats, carbohydrates, vitamins and minerals. Kim gets her nutrients from all the different types of foods she eats. Each nutrient has a particular job to do.

Proteins are found in foods like fish, meat, nuts, beans, cheese and eggs. Proteins help build Kim's body. Her bones, muscles and skin are made up mainly of proteins. Proteins also give Kim energy and help her body to heal and repair itself when it is damaged.

Fats are found in many foods such as butter, oils, cheese, milk, meat and nuts. Fats help Kim's body to keep itself warm. They are also necessary for some of the vitamins to do their work.

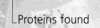

└Proteins found in foods such as meat and fish help to build Kim's body

Carbohydrates, found in bread, cereal, rice, pasta and potatoes, give Kim most of her energy. Fibre is the part of a carbohydrate food that cannot be digested. Fibre helps Kim's body to move the food through her intestine.

Kim's body also needs vitamins and minerals to work properly and to grow.

9

Kim's tummy is rumbling. She stopped eating lunch weeks ago.

In the evenings she eats salad with her meal – like Carol, she has no bread or potatoes. To take her mind off eating, she goes to her room to do some extra school work.

'Come and watch TV with me,' says Carol one evening. Kim thinks of the old days. She used to lie on the sofa with Angie, munching crisps while they watched their favourite soap. But Angie is out now with her boyfriend, Harry. Kim shakes her head.

'I've got too much to do,' she tells Carol, as she picks up her bag.

In her room, Kim tries to work but she can't stop thinking about food. She has a headache.

After school on Friday, Kim goes shopping with Angie and Carol. They are choosing Kim's outfit for the wedding.

Kim pulls on a tight skirt. It's a size ten – and the zip does up easily. Kim pads out of the changing room in her bare feet and parades in front of Carol and Angie. 'You look great!' they tell her.

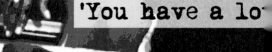

'You have a lo

10

This pyramid shows how much of a particular food it is healthy to eat. Carbohydrates, fruit and vegetables are at the bottom of the pyramid because they are the foods you need to eat most of. Oils and fats are at the top because you only need small amounts of these.

dieting

Dieting and the body

When Kim's body needs more food, chemicals in her brain increase to give her an appetite. Kim feels hungry. Her brain sends messages to other parts of her body to prepare them for her next meal. Kim's mouth becomes wet with saliva, her stomach juices get ready to work. If Kim doesn't eat, or doesn't eat enough, her brain keeps sending 'time to eat' messages and producing the chemicals which make her appetite work. Pictures of hot, buttered toast float in and out of Kim's mind. Her hungry brain never stops reminding her about food.

Like everyone on a strict diet, Kim soon feels the effects of too little food. She becomes tired and is unable to concentrate. In the short term, Kim's diet makes her feel uncomfortable. In the long term, it may rob her of some of the valuable nutrients her growing body needs.

11

igure,' says the shop assistant. Kim glows with pleasure.

What is a calorie?
A calorie is a unit of energy. Everything you eat contains calories. Your body uses calories for everything it does – breathing, digesting food, even sleeping. You are burning up calories just by reading this book.

Kim stands in front of the mirror in her room. She frowns as she checks her body.

'My bottom still looks fat,' she thinks.

She gets on to the bathroom scales.

'I'll just lose a bit more weight,' Kim tells herself with determination.

Over the next few weeks, Kim cuts down on her breakfast. Most days she has one piece of toast with low-fat spread. She's given up taking milk in her tea.

When the family eats together, Kim panics at the thought of having to manage a whole plate of food. She picks at the meal in front of her. Some evenings, when no one is looking, she scoops her meal into the bin.

Although Kim isn't eating much herself, she has started to cook for her family. Tonight she's made lasagne topped with piles of grated cheese. A few shreds of cheese have fallen on to the work surface. Kim's stomach growls and she longs to stuff them into her mouth.

'No, Kim!' she warns herself. 'You're too fat already.'

At the table Kim serves everyone a plateful of lasagne – and helps herself only to the vegetables.

'Mmm, delicious!' says Carol. 'It's full of calories, but it's worth breaking my diet for! Where's yours, Kim?'

'I picked at it in the kitchen. I'm full already!' lies Kim as she watches her family tuck in.

Kim hasn't had a prope

what is an eating disorder?

Kim's diet is turning into something else. She is beginning to develop an eating disorder. People with an eating disorder may eat far too little or much too much. There are many reasons why people develop an eating disorder. They are often sad, angry or very confused about all or some part of their lives. They use food to try to cope with their lives, which they feel are out of control.

Eating disorders are not caused by slimming. They can often begin with a slimming diet, but usually they are about trying to cope with problems that have nothing to do with food.

13

eal for weeks.

Claire catches up with Kim one day after school.

'I hardly see you now!' Claire complains. 'You're always too busy working. We're supposed to be friends.'

'Find another friend then!' snaps Kim, turning away towards home. She shivers in the spring sunshine. Kim feels the cold a lot these days.

'Aren't you coming to tennis practice?' asks Claire.

'I've dropped out of the team,' Kim tells her. 'Mrs Lewis said it was OK.'

Claire is worried about her friend. She puts her arm around Kim's shoulder.

'Kim, you've lost a lot of weight!' Claire blurts out. She's shocked at how bony Kim feels. 'Does your mum know you're not eating lunch?'

'I'm FAT – and it's none of your business anyway!' shouts Kim, beginning to cry.

She hurries of

The eating disorder Kim is developing is called anorexia nervosa. People with this illness cut down on their food so much that they starve. Sometimes they make themselves sick after they have eaten. Losing weight becomes the only control they feel they have over their lives.

As her eating disorder develops, lots of changes take place in Kim. Some of these changes take place in her mind. Kim has become secretive about food. She eats only certain foods, often in a certain order. She is well below a healthy weight, but her mind tells her she looks fat.

Other changes take place throughout Kim's body. A chemical called adrenaline, produced in her kidneys, pumps into Kim's brain. This makes her very active and causes her to feel 'high' and powerful. It's a bit like taking a drug. Slowly, the longer Kim starves herself, the more she needs to starve to get this same feeling. Because she isn't having enough food, Kim's digestion has slowed down. She is constipated, her stomach is tight, sore and swollen.

what is anorexia?

15

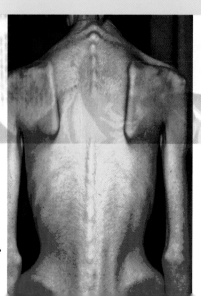

Extreme cases of anorexia nervosa can lead to death.

nd Claire stares after her.

Without enough fat to provide warmth, Kim feels cold. Lacking food, Kim's brain has more and more difficulty concentrating. It is becoming hard for her to read or have a conversation – or even to sleep. Kim's illness causes her to draw away from her friends. She feels sad and lonely. Her only aim in life is to lose more weight.

'You're so fat!' she sobs to her skinny reflection.

Kim finds all sorts of reasons for not eating with her family. Today Carol and Joe insist that she sit down with them for a meal.

'We're all eating together this evening. No excuses,' says her dad. 'We hardly see you these days, Kim.'

'And you're getting very thin,' says Kim's mum peering across at her.

'Get off my back!' thinks Kim.

The food seems to stick in Kim's throat. She cuts it into tiny pieces and moves it around her plate. Suddenly she feels panicky. She can't eat any more.

'I had a big lunch. I'm full,' she says, pushing her plate away.

Instead of playing tennis with the team, Kim goes running on her own.

She runs every evening after school. First she checks her weight on the bathroom scales. Then she runs five times round the park. Back at home she weighs herself again before doing her stomach exercises. Up and down, up and down she goes, until she is exhausted.

'Burn those calories, Kim!' she whispers.

Her body aches, but her brain feels as if it's floating. Kim returns to the mirror again and again.

Later, in her room

Burning up energy

Kim's exercise routine is part of her effort to lose weight. As she moves her muscles in hard exercise, they start to burn up more energy as fuel. When Kim is running, her muscles are using at least

As Kim exercises, chemicals called endorphins are pumped through her body.

exercise

twenty times more energy than usual, burning carbohydrates and stored fat. The star jumps burn up much, much more.

Some other things happen too. As Kim exercises long and hard, chemicals called endorphins – the body's natural painkillers – are pumped into her bloodstream. Endorphins dull the pain of Kim's aching muscles and let her carry on exercising for longer. Endorphins also give Kim a huge rush of well-being. This is combined with the powerful feeling of control over her body that exercise gives her. Hard exercise gives Kim such a burst of good feelings that she wants to do more and more.

im does twenty star jumps. Then she weighs herself st one more time before she crawls into bed.

17

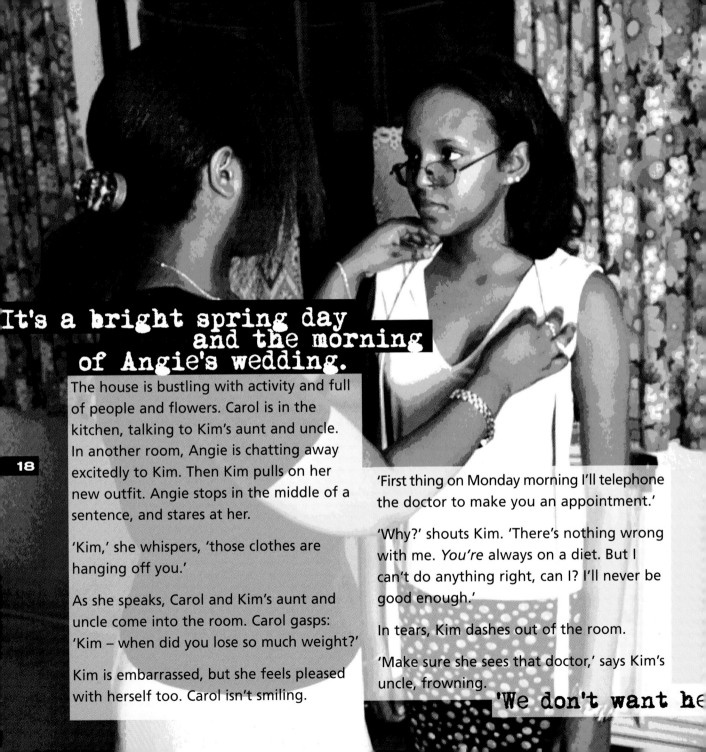

It's a bright spring day and the morning of Angie's wedding.

The house is bustling with activity and full of people and flowers. Carol is in the kitchen, talking to Kim's aunt and uncle. In another room, Angie is chatting away excitedly to Kim. Then Kim pulls on her new outfit. Angie stops in the middle of a sentence, and stares at her.

'Kim,' she whispers, 'those clothes are hanging off you.'

As she speaks, Carol and Kim's aunt and uncle come into the room. Carol gasps: 'Kim – when did you lose so much weight?'

Kim is embarrassed, but she feels pleased with herself too. Carol isn't smiling.

'First thing on Monday morning I'll telephone the doctor to make you an appointment.'

'Why?' shouts Kim. 'There's nothing wrong with me. *You're* always on a diet. But I can't do anything right, can I? I'll never be good enough.'

In tears, Kim dashes out of the room.

'Make sure she sees that doctor,' says Kim's uncle, frowning.

'We don't want he

Long-term damage

Kim feels 'high' from over-exercising. She gets an adrenaline rush from under-eating. Together, they give her a powerful and speedy feeling of control. If she carries on, Kim may become trapped in a circle of starvation, exercise, and more starvation – and find herself unable to stop.

Lack of nourishment over a period of time is a serious risk to health. Starvation changes the levels of chemicals called hormones in the body. In girls this causes their breasts to stop growing and their periods to stop or never start. Boys, too, will stop growing and developing until their diet improves.

Starvation can lead to a condition where the bones become thin and easily broken. Many people who have recovered from anorexia may get bone problems when they are older. Without a healthy supply of vitamins and minerals, the kidneys are unable to do their job. People with anorexia also face the risk of long-term damage to their kidneys.

If the human body doesn't get enough food to keep it going, it begins to waste away. It breaks down the protein in its muscles to use as fuel. The heart is a muscle. People with anorexia are in danger of weakening their hearts and may even die of a heart attack.

19

wasting away

tarving herself to death.'

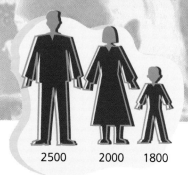

Adults and children need to eat a certain amount of calories every day to stay healthy.

2500   2000   1800

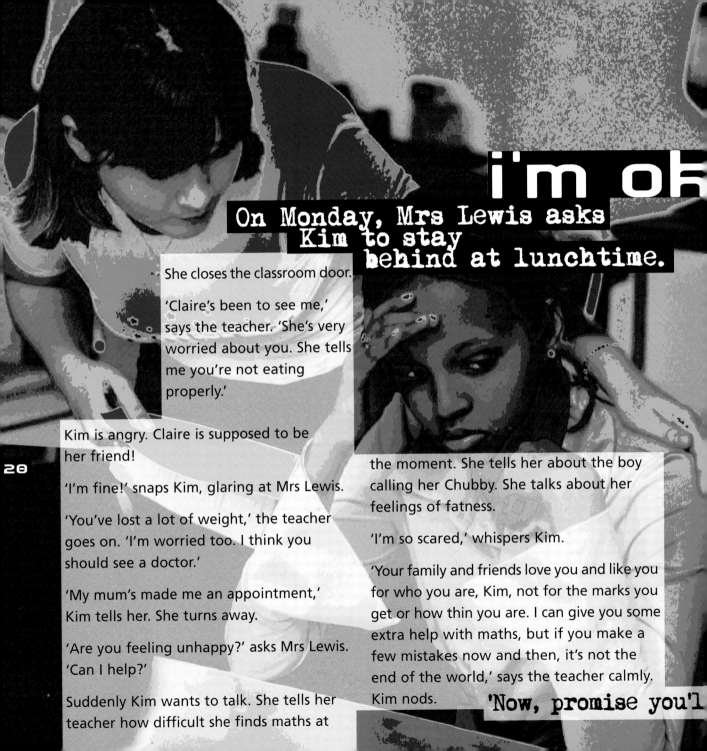

On Monday, Mrs Lewis asks Kim to stay behind at lunchtime.

She closes the classroom door.

'Claire's been to see me,' says the teacher. 'She's very worried about you. She tells me you're not eating properly.'

Kim is angry. Claire is supposed to be her friend!

'I'm fine!' snaps Kim, glaring at Mrs Lewis.

'You've lost a lot of weight,' the teacher goes on. 'I'm worried too. I think you should see a doctor.'

'My mum's made me an appointment,' Kim tells her. She turns away.

'Are you feeling unhappy?' asks Mrs Lewis. 'Can I help?'

Suddenly Kim wants to talk. She tells her teacher how difficult she finds maths at the moment. She tells her about the boy calling her Chubby. She talks about her feelings of fatness.

'I'm so scared,' whispers Kim.

'Your family and friends love you and like you for who you are, Kim, not for the marks you get or how thin you are. I can give you some extra help with maths, but if you make a few mistakes now and then, it's not the end of the world,' says the teacher calmly. Kim nods.

'Now, promise you'l

you're ok

The pressures of growing up

Kim's teacher is telling her that she's fine, just as she is. For some young people, the stresses of growing up can seem too great at times. Like Kim, they may lose confidence in themselves. It can seem that the only thing they are good at controlling is what they eat. They then judge themselves on how much they have eaten or how much weight they have lost.

Kim needs to learn that people like her for who she is inside. She needs to learn to like herself too.

If you are low in confidence, you can learn to improve your feelings about yourself. Remember, no one's good at everything. Try something new. Sport is a great way to be with others and keep healthy at the same time. Or you might try dancing – or drama – or conservation work! Look in the local paper or library or on the internet to find out what's going on where you live.

If your worries are getting on top of you, tell someone. If you can't talk to your parents, find a teacher or another adult you trust.

Young people have a lot of pressures to deal with. They are beginning to look and feel like adults, but their parents may still be treating them as children. On top of this, there are the pressures of a new school, exams and, later on, the choice of a career. It's no wonder that young people are sometimes scared and confused.

When you're growing and developing your body may feel bulky and awkward for a time. This is normal. It needs a little while before it settles into its new shape. You can help it along with healthy food and exercise.

ee a doctor, won't you?' Kim agrees.

21

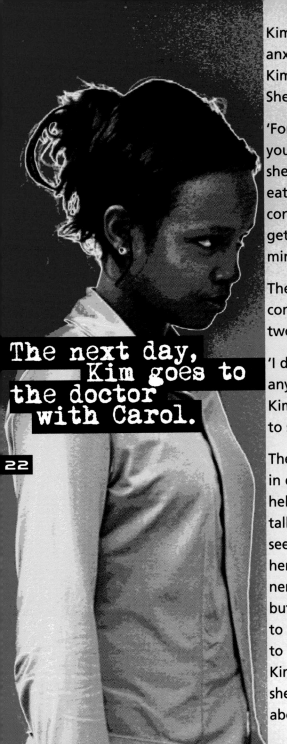

Kim feels scared and anxious. The doctor checks Kim's weight and height. She turns to Kim.

'For a girl of your height you are very underweight,' she says. 'You have to try to eat more sensibly. I'm also concerned that you aren't getting the vitamins and minerals you need.'

The doctor asks Kim to come back to see her in two weeks.

'I don't want you to lose any more weight,' she tells Kim firmly. 'I'd also like you to see a therapist.'

The therapist is a specialist in eating disorders. She will help Kim by listening and talking to her. Kim goes to see the therapist with both her parents. At first she is nervous and embarrassed, but the therapist is easy to talk to. She asks Kim to call her Jenny. Soon Kim is saying how scared she feels about life and about putting on weight.

She explains how worried she is about her school work. She tells her parents and Jenny how much she is going to miss her sister. And Kim wonders how her mum will cope when she leaves home too.

There's a lo

Diana, Princess of Wales,
drew the public's attention to eating disorders when she discussed
her own struggle with bulimia.

getting help

Other eating disorders

Two other eating disorders that Jenny helps with are bulimia nervosa and compulsive eating disorder. Like people with anorexia, people who have bulimia nervosa are afraid of becoming fat. But people with bulimia have powerful urges to overeat. They force down huge amounts of food in a very short space of time, not caring what it is or what it tastes like. This is called binge eating and is done in secret.

To control their weight, they may then try to get rid of all the food by making themselves sick. People with this eating disorder usually feel disgusted with themselves after a binge. They may punish themselves by eating very little or nothing at all for a time, until the next binge.

People with compulsive eating disorder or binge-eating disorder think about food a lot of the time and feel out of control with food. They may overeat in secret or pick at food all day long.

Damage from bulimia
People who suffer from bulimia can harm their health. Their eating habits may give them stomach cramps, constipation and diarrhoea. Being sick (vomiting) over and over again brings acid up from their stomachs, which damages their teeth. Vomiting like this can also lead to the loss of important minerals from the body.

23

o talk about.
Kim will need to visit the
therapist again and again.

Late in the autumn term, Kim is back in the tennis team. She talks to Claire in the changing rooms.

'It feels weird to be wearing these clothes again,' she tells her friend, as she pulls on her kit. 'They almost fit now – I must have put on some more weight since last week.'

Claire looks at her carefully. 'Don't start that again,' she begs her friend.

'No. I'm OK, ' Kim reassures her. 'But I can't just click out of it, you know. It's really hard for me to let myself get heavier.'

Kim has been seeing Jenny every week all through the summer. The therapist has explained that it may be a long time before Kim can really relax about her weight. Kim has become more confident. It helps her to talk about her problems with Jenny. When something is getting on top of her, she knows she can talk it through with Mrs Lewis, too.

Just then Mrs Lewis comes over to the girls. She is smiling.

'It's good to have you back in the team, Kim!' the teacher says.

'It's good to be back

Growing needs

When you are young you are growing fast, so you need more energy and greater amounts of some nutrients than an adult would. During teenage years, the mineral iron is very important for

getting better

muscle development and general growth. If you don't get enough iron in your diet you will begin to feel weak and tired.

25

Try to eat breakfast cereals that have added iron (you could eat them as snacks, if you don't want them at breakfast time). Eat them with a glass of fruit juice containing vitamin C, which will help your body take in the iron.

aughs Kim, and she means it.

Your bones are growing incredibly fast too, so you need lots more calcium than your parents do. You can get this mineral from milk, cheese, yogurt, bread, dried fruits, nuts and green, leafy vegetables.

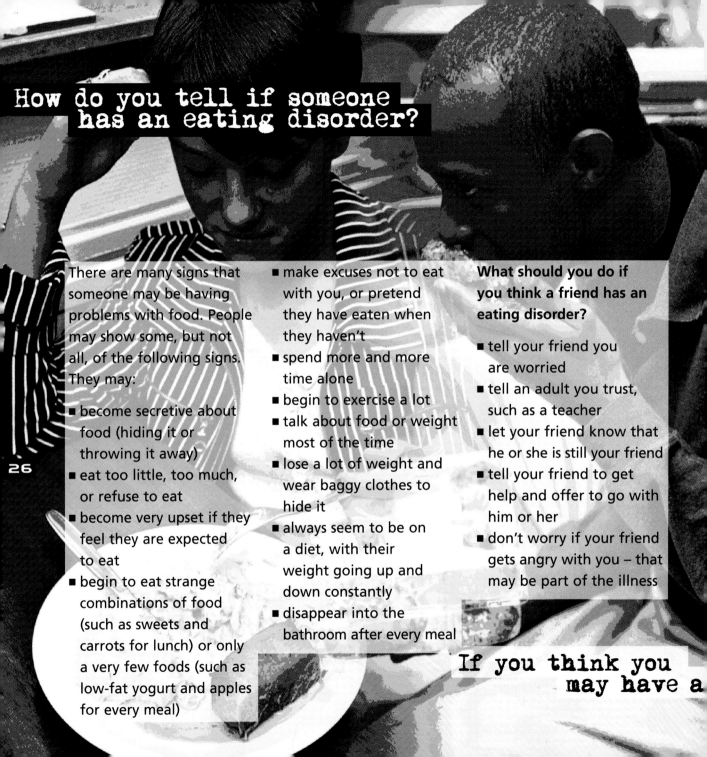

How do you tell if someone has an eating disorder?

There are many signs that someone may be having problems with food. People may show some, but not all, of the following signs. They may:

- become secretive about food (hiding it or throwing it away)
- eat too little, too much, or refuse to eat
- become very upset if they feel they are expected to eat
- begin to eat strange combinations of food (such as sweets and carrots for lunch) or only a very few foods (such as low-fat yogurt and apples for every meal)
- make excuses not to eat with you, or pretend they have eaten when they haven't
- spend more and more time alone
- begin to exercise a lot
- talk about food or weight most of the time
- lose a lot of weight and wear baggy clothes to hide it
- always seem to be on a diet, with their weight going up and down constantly
- disappear into the bathroom after every meal

What should you do if you think a friend has an eating disorder?

- tell your friend you are worried
- tell an adult you trust, such as a teacher
- let your friend know that he or she is still your friend
- tell your friend to get help and offer to go with him or her
- don't worry if your friend gets angry with you – that may be part of the illness

If you think you may have a

eating disorders
the signs

How do you help a friend get better?
People with eating disorders have to face up to their problems. They have to want to get better. You can't do it for them, and it can take a long time. But you can help by:

- sharing your feelings with them and listening if they want to share theirs
- trying not to talk about food or weight, especially their weight
- not treating your friend as an ill person
- talking it through with an adult you trust

Do you have an eating disorder?
If you do some of the following things, you may have a problem with food. Do you:

- think about food a lot of the time and panic about your weight?
- feel out of control about food?

- feel scared of eating or that you don't deserve to eat?
- feel guilty about what you have eaten?
- overeat in secret?
- avoid eating?
- make yourself sick after a meal?
- lie about the amount you've eaten?
- always try to lose weight or stop putting on weight?

ating disorder, get help now.
Talk to someone you trust –
a teacher, a parent or a friend.

Facts about weight and dieting

- Being thin doesn't make you happy
- Everyone needs about 1,000 calories a day just to be able to sleep. You need lots more for all the other things you do in your life
- Weighing yourself every day doesn't make you slimmer

- Teenage slimming is a bad idea. Your body is growing and changing. If you do want to diet, wait until you are older
- Dieting makes you feel weak and dizzy
- Dieting can give you bad breath
- Dieting can make you constipated

- Between 95 per cent and 98 per cent of all dieters put all their lost weight back on again. 50 per cent put back more weight than they lost in the first place!

Facts about eating disorders

- Boys get eating disorders too – 10 per cent of sufferers are male
- Eating disorders can ruin your teeth and gums
- Eating disorders can make your hair fall out
- Eating disorders can harm your body – girls need their body weight to be made up of 15-18 per cent fat if they are to grow breasts and have a baby one day
- Starving bodies may try to keep warm with a layer of fine hair, which grows on the face, shoulders and back
- Untreated anorexia can lead to death

health facts

29

US gymnast Christy Henrich's heart was weakened by anorexia nervosa. She died of a heart attack, aged 22.

glossary

anorexia nervosa people suffering from anorexia nervosa starve themselves and lose a dangerous amount of weight.

bulimia nervosa people suffering from bulimia nervosa eat a large amount of food all at once and may then try to get rid of it by vomiting.

calorie a unit of energy; everything we eat contains calories and everything we do uses them up.

carbohydrates the starches and sugars in food which give you energy.

compulsive eating disorder also called binge-eating disorder. People suffering from compulsive eating disorder pick at food all day long, overeat in secret or feel they are unable to control their food intake.

fats nutrients your body needs for energy, warmth and to take in some kinds of vitamins.

fibre the part of a carbohydrate food which cannot be digested, for example potato skins and sweetcorn husks. Our bodies need fibre to help move food through the intestine.

minerals nutrients taken up from the earth by plants; when we eat these plants, in the form of fruit, vegetables and pulses, the nutrients enter our bodies as food.

nutrients chemical substances found in food; our bodies need these in order to grow, to keep healthy and for energy.

proteins nutrients that our bodies need for growth and repair.

therapist a person trained and skilled in treating illnesses of the mind or body by talking and listening.

vitamins nutrients that our bodies need in small amounts. There are thirteen vitamins.

further information

Getting Help

If you have a problem with food and eating there are people who can help. Talk to an adult you trust. Go to your doctor. You could also phone one of the organisations listed below. Sometimes the telephone lines are busy. If they are, don't give up – keep trying.

Eating Disorders Association

Youthline 01603 765050

ChildLine

Freephone 0800 1111

The Samaritans

08457 909090

Websites

The following websites have information about eating disorders:

http://www.edauk.com
(Eating Disorders Association)

http://www.childline.org.uk

index